Praise for *Last Day on Earth in the Eternal City*

Reading a poem by Angie Estes is like listening in on the intricate turnings and realizations of a brilliant mind, a mind that follows one path only to discover another more surprising one, a mind that observes with an acuteness and intelligence I can only envy. In *Last Day on Earth in the Eternal City,* Estes is at the height of her power: erudite and intimate, playful and musical. But there is gravity here, as well, beneath the slipperiness of language — a sense of the profound presence of our cultural pasts, the seductiveness of image and language, the power of romantic longing, connection, and loss. I've admired Estes' work for decades — and this may be my favorite of her books.

Kevin Prufer

An electric intelligence courses through Angie Estes' new poems. As soon as I opened the book I knew I was in for a ride. There's a worldliness about the poems that gives them heft and authority, while simultaneously enhancing their intimacy, eroticism, and spontaneity. Linguistically playful (in several languages!), lively on the page, funny and unpredictable, these poems range through the worlds of art, music, politics, science, you name it, with a probing curiosity that's irresistible. They also teach the reader how to read them, which is a quality I greatly admire, and which only great poetry possesses.

Chase Twichell

Angie Estes' poems sing life most gloriously — the sensual and the sacred; art's intensity and the earthly everyday; language, music and meaning. This beautiful collection, filled with wonders, exhilarates.

Claire Messud

Moving between artistic/literary history and the perils of human desire, Angie Estes' *Last Day on Earth in the Eternal City* achieves a vast poetic range and resonance: "Like Huck, I *reckon I got to light out / for the Territory,* out where you knew the way / to my house the way a blood clot / knows the way to a heart." She's one of the best poets of her generation, one whose diction operates at the highest and most complex level of tri-lingual improvisation. Her work "privileges [our] vocabulary." *Last Day on Earth in the Eternal City* flashes perilously like "the dorsal fin of some / *fin de siècle.*"

Mark Irwin

Angie Estes writes poems for grown-ups, especially grown-ups who share her sensibility, which is at once passionate, intellectual, questing, cultured, and attuned to the worlds of nature, eros, art, and books. She does not shy away from her learning, but she wears it lightly. She explores the world by exploring language. Her poetic lines — sometimes long, or divided, sometimes abbreviated, or stair-stepped — signal a mind searching, discovering, pausing, and then continuing, a mind in the act of discovery and invention. Describing her own art, she modifies Proust: "the shape / of the sentence is the shape / of thought." No one writing poetry today manages to unite intellect and sensuousness so deftly as she does.

Willard Spiegelman

In Angie Estes' extraordinary book, poems invite us across white space like water-striders as words or images reappear in unexpected ways. Allusions abound across time and space — Proust, Twain, Thelonious Monk, Giotto, Tosca, *The Pillow Book* — and imbedded in this culturally polyglot matrix is a lost love. Restless yet elegant, the orchestral arrangement of images and language evokes both passion and loss. So many facets: this is a glittering gem of a book.

Pamela Alexander

Neruda, Glück, Tranströmer, Bishop ... and, yes, Angie Estes, a poet who to my mind is their equal. At once propulsive and recursive, wildly erudite and supremely sensual, these are revelatory poems in the way we find in "Dark Matter":

... for Leonardo

sfumato is not something you do to

a painting but something you do

to the viewer, each layer a disappearing

veil:

Which is to say poems (like the title of the book itself) that delight again and again in profound and playful paradox, their mysteries both timeless and precisely occasional, as if announced in the voice of an oracle or a 10th century mystic via a battered drive-in movie speaker. Which is to say, Estes at the peak of her powers — and what powers to behold.

Daniel Lawless

Previous Praise

Whenever I see a poem by Angie Estes I prepare myself for serious delight. Her timing and her ever-uninhibited instinct for poetic shape are the triumphs of a first-rate musical intelligence. Angie Estes is Fred Astaire and Ginger too: backwards in high heels, forward on rollerskates, never have classy and sexy been better matched.

Linda Gregerson

Angie Estes has recently created some of the most beautiful verbal objects on the planet.

Stephanie Burt

This is a poetry of style, elegance, and fresh surprise, for the ear and the eye, the heart and the mind. It reminds me why I read.

Langdon Hammer

Last Day on Earth in the Eternal City

Last Day on Earth in the Eternal City

Angie Estes

ed.

UNBOUND EDITION PRESS

Atlanta

FIRST EDITION

Printed in the United States of America

LIBRARY OF CONGRESS RECORD

Name: Estes, Angie, author.
Title: Last Day on Earth in the Eternal City / Angie Estes.
Edition: First edition.
Published: Atlanta : Unbound Edition Press, 2025.

LCCN: 2024946028
LCCN Permalink: https://lccn.loc.gov/2024946028
ISBN: 979-8-9906141-7-8 (fine softcover)

Designed by Eleanor Safe and Joseph Floresca
Printed by Bookmobile, Minneapolis, MN
Distributed by Itasca Books

123456789

Unbound Edition Press
1270 Caroline Street, Suite D120
Box 448
Atlanta, GA 30307

Contents

Last Day on Earth in the Eternal City

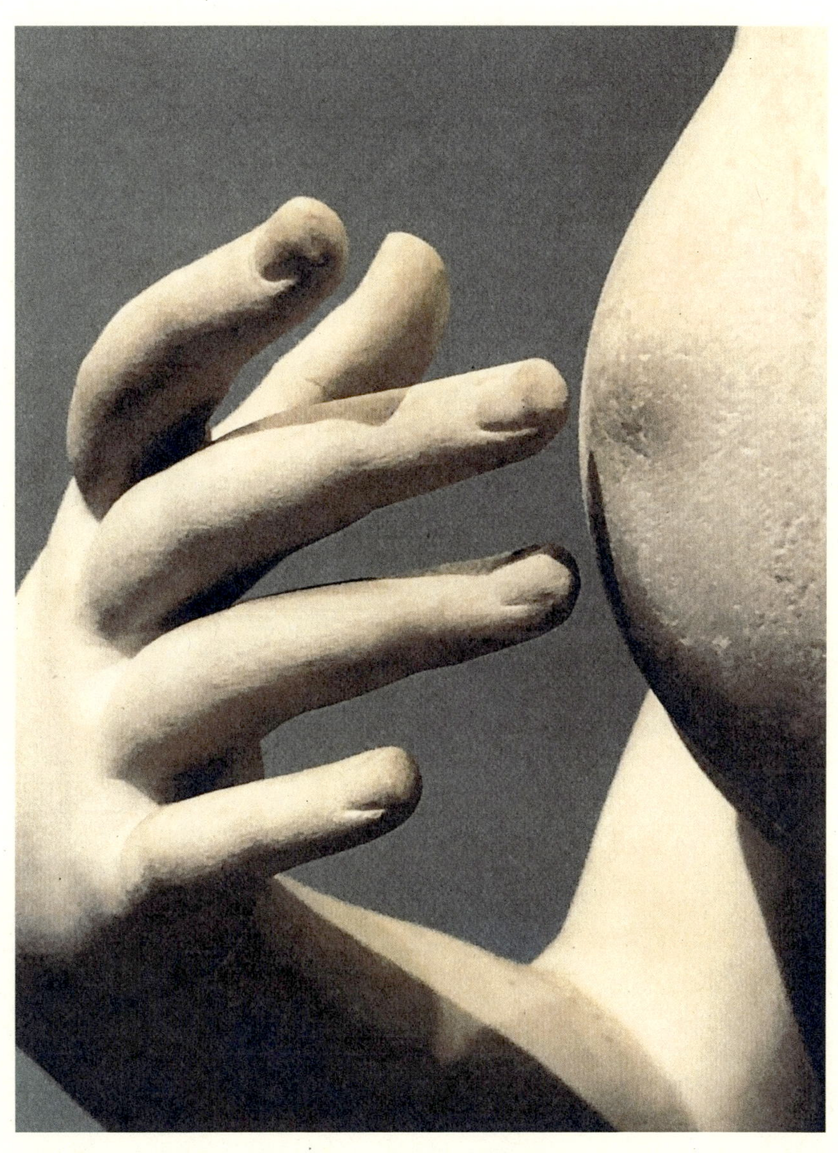

And so we ought not to fear in love, as in everyday life, the future alone, but even the past, which often comes to life for us only when the future has come and gone — and not only the past which we discover after the event but the past which we have long kept stored within ourselves and suddenly learn how to interpret.

Marcel Proust, *In Search of Lost Time*

I am wedged between two tenses: you have gone (which I lament), you are here (since I am addressing you).

Roland Barthes, *A Lover's Discourse*

The summer after the war in Ukraine began, she said: *the cherries will be ripe, but there will be no one there to pick them ...*

The Swallows Come Out

like stars, wallowing
in the dim evening light
because in the country
of blue, at times even
the borders of the heart
are the borders one needs
to leave. So I waited
at the airport, a woman beneath
a sign that said *Gate B hold* — what
Heloise and Abelard must have
been feeling when
they named their son Astrolabe,
an instrument for
determining one's position
in the universe. The room where
they met in secret was not
far from *Pont Neuf,* the "new bridge,"
which is the oldest bridge
in Paris, and like the French
grammatical liaison, it puts
something hard, something voiced
between two vowels: like the sound
you make when I am finally
inside you. It's the way
scientists knew they had discovered
a new group of blue whales: they
were singing a song no one
had ever heard.

Inside Hagia Sophia,

above the southwest entrance, Justinian,
                    on the left of the Virgin in the mosaic, offers her
Hagia Sophia, which holds the mosaic. On the right,

Constantine holds out to her Constantinople, which
                    contains Hagia Sophia. Small African birds known as
honeyguides — skilled at locating beehives

but unable to break into them to feed — attract
                    humans with a call and then lead the way. For three
million years, people have opened

and emptied the hives, leaving just enough
                    for the birds to keep them coming back
to call again like some almost immaculate

conception or *mise-en-abîme* in which one places
                    a copy of an image within the image itself
to make an infinite sequence. Signs posted

in the Paris metro say *Attentif ensemble!*
                    reminding us to be watchful together, apparently
against the appearance of whoever is not

watchful with us. Remember when
                    we used to be able to call collect, sometimes
even person-to-person? And there was

a party line, not the one we'd have to
                    walk, but the one we'd listen in on: holding
the hard black receiver to the ear

was like watching della Francesca's *Madonna*
                del Parto unbutton her dress only to find inside
another Madonna unbuttoning

her dress, like watching the dead flying
                like wild geese through fog: there, not-there, there, not-
there. Not there, yet all the while you hear them.

Privilege for the vocabulary

Among random entries scattered

on Galileo's shopping list for making

a telescope: something specific but not

relevant for the instrument — and by no means

something you could shop for, like Tosca's dress

which you're re-designing for a more

voluptuous soprano, just as you let out the seams

of this poem. *O reason not the need*

and *I know not seems,* but still one wants

to know what kind of thing this thing is.

Turns out it's not a song by Cole Porter

but a reminder to obtain the authorization

to publish the first dictionary, *vocabolario,*

of the Italian language: a *privilegio* attached to

the list as if it were a ledge to hold onto

or jump off of, as if just the right word, *le mot*

juste, could split open the heavens the way

you open beneath me and speak

rapid Russian phrases that I — a woman

stitched to Earth and one worn

language — will never know the meaning of.

The Present

was tense, the past

was here, the air so warm and waft

you could toss it around your neck

like a scarf, like the lambs

from the island of Ouessant

off the coast of Brest — *pré-salé,*

salt meadow — fed on sea-salted grass

so that their flesh becomes tender

while their hearts are still

pumping. According to the Talmud,

it is better to wish that

you had never been born

than to think of what's above, what's

below, what's behind, what's

ahead. But still on the hills above

Ōtsuchi, on the coast of northern

Japan, with an old-fashioned black

telephone connected to nothing, nowhere,

the living make phone calls

to the dead, just as God himself

when he's alone sits way up

in the top corner "bird's nest" seats

of the Opéra Garnier in Paris — from where

he sees the stage only if he stands

and leans to the side — and sings,

Vous me with that vous-do that you

do so well.

I Can't See the Hour,

Non vedo l'ora,

is what they say in

Italy when they want

to say *I can't wait*

because translation is

borrowed language at

best, and best when it

takes the advice of

Thelonius Monk: "Don't

play *everything*

(or everytime) ... Some music

just imagined ... " the way

that bumblebees at

evening curl into

purple blossoms of thistle

and imagine the heat

that will stir them

in the morning and I

wake in the night next

to you and say *I can't see*

the hour

because the night

is *borrowed time, borrowed*

summer: the entire month

of September when everyone

else has gone back to

work and we go

to the Black Sea and the water

is still warm.

Dark Matter

St. Francis preached to the birds, although

we're not exactly sure, of course,

what he told them. We do know

that he once said, "Speak the gospel

continuously; if necessary, use

words," but in Giotto's painting,

the birds seem to be

listening intently, still silent.

But wouldn't you like to know

what the Gray Catbirds are

talking about in their early morning

klatch, their vowels like car wheels taking

a corner too fast? Or why crows feel

the need to comment on

everything? And wouldn't it be

amazing if I could tell you

in this poem? I wonder

whether St. Francis ever preached

to deer. I never hear them say

anything, and they seem so content

munching away and glistening

in the spring green field. This poem

would like to know what

color they are: honey or

sherry? I can't decide, although

I've finally figured out why I feel

you so intensely when you're

not here: cosmologists tell us that

24 percent of our universe is composed

of dark matter, which like every other

kind of matter exerts and responds

to gravity, but does not interact

with light, which makes it invisible

and extremely difficult to

detect. We know that Leonardo

was a genius because way back

in 1472 he knew that the way to

create mystery, complexity, and intimacy

in a painting was by means of

sfumato, making something vanish

like smoke. So he applied layer

after layer of varnish, each

layer sifting light and

dark, because for Leonardo

sfumato is not something you do to

a painting but something you do

to the viewer, each layer a disappearing

veil: as the Virgin reads

in Leonardo's *Annunciation,* the miracle

is that the dark words

become light

as the pages turn

invisible.

Le principal trait de mon caractère:

desire to see the back

side of things since

the back is the only part

of our body that we can

barely see or touch,

to taste the difference

between Burgundy wines

grown *au-dessus* or *au-dessous.* Even

in the Scuola Grande di

San Rocco in Venice, we walked

holding mirrors

in order to better see

Tintoretto's paintings

on the ceiling. Think of how

the trunk of the paperbark

maple bursts into flames

when the sun sneaks up

behind it. Tall stones are known

as *menhir* in Welsh, *hir*

meaning long as in

hiraeth, nostalgia or longing

for home. But the backside

of nostalgia — *nostos,* return,
and the desire to return —

also bears *algos,* pain, the im-
possibility of returning. When I was

a child, I wanted to find a way
to take the blue-, pink-, and

yellow-dyed rabbits' feet
hanging from belt loops or rear-view

mirrors and give them back
to the hopping rabbits.

And I loved the Biblical story
of the many loves

of bread, although in hindsight
I see they must have been

loaves. Remember the moment
in *Le grand blond avec une chaussure*

noire when Mireille Darc
greets her paramour at midnight

in a high-necked silk, black
velvet dress and then pivots

to walk away, revealing
that the dress has

no back? The moon, too,
sometimes goes black

just before slipping out
of its eclipse. In front of

the homestead where my
family lived in the Blue Ridge Mountains,

beyond trees and thickets,
an occasional upright

stone, a row of jonquils
blooms each spring. Sometimes

we cut them early and
arrange them in a vase: you love

to count the hours it takes
them to open. Now, at this

moment, when everything is
still possible, I remember you

as you will be.

Yours truly,

It was the best of times, it was

the worst of times: every book I had

ever read came back

to read me, along with the 474,500

migrating birds that, according to

Birdcast, have crossed over Champaign County

flying south, so far tonight: American Redstarts,

Swainson's Thrushes, Gray Catbirds, White-crowned

Sparrows, Rose-breasted Grosbeaks. Even now

325,500 birds are in flight at an attitude,

I mean altitude, of 1,700 feet

and a speed of 27 mph, while across the Atlantic

at Paris Fashion Week, two men waving

canisters of Fabrican's liquid fiber

circle and spray a dress onto an almost

naked model. When the white downy sheath

is complete, another woman steps forward

and shapes shoulder straps with her hands, sliding them

off the shoulders before cutting a slit

up one leg from floor to thigh. Still,

so many questions: will I love you forever

or leave you forever? And will forever be long enough

to do both? Like Huck, *I reckon I got to light out*

for the Territory, out where you knew the way

to my house the way a blood clot

knows the way to a heart.

Spring

Everything is in such a

hurry, even though I'm sure

Faulkner was right when he said

the past is never dead; it's not even

past. One day the Serviceberry tree

flashes red and yellow

with Cedar Waxwings, and the next —

nothing but leaves. The squirrel

lies in a bright red halo

of blood on the asphalt, its right arm

still running, even as the halos of martyred

saints Cosmas and Damian keep

rolling with their heads

in Fra Angelico's painting. If they were in

Japan, they could be put back

together like broken pieces

of porcelain, *kintsugi,* repaired with

a thick seam of lacquer

and gold: the past could be

morning sky or evening sky, even

Evensong — golden caviar on

buttered toast — as if *Louvre*

and *velour* had suddenly turned

into each other. The past

is so unwilling to stay

where we put it that we had

to give it its own conjugated

tense, *past imperfect,* in which

no matter what may happen, the past

continues — as in *je désirais*: the condition

was never-ending.

Le don de la nature que je voudrais avoir:

Interior, Sunlight on the Floor, a door,
a window made of four windows, each
with six panes, not counting
the panes of sunlight
on the floor. So is the painting
a tarnished gold interior or
a landscape of the French
word *hôte,* both host and guest, subject
and object — or what's in
between: the margin,
that which holds the book
together. You would
look and I'd always
be there. I would chant
my mother's favorite
sayings: *I have a sneaking suspicion,*
That's what I thought, You'll do
no such thing, and she
would appear.
Hammershoi painted room
after room, empty
or with one woman
viewed from behind, while
Hans Hartung and Anna-Eva Bergman
designed their villa in Antibes
with windows the dimensions of
paintings, white exterior walls
where light and shadow could continue
to make new designs. Hartung saved
his spattered wooden closet doors
and papered the floors in order

to preserve the overspray
because what was left over, accidental,
was as important as what was
purposeful, meant. I'd gather
all the words not used at the end
of the poem, and that would
be the poem: bespoke galore, intimate
in time, a late sun-split field.

You Had Me at *Premier Cru,*

you had me on the hillside

of *Clos de la Croix de Pierre* in Burgundy

even though we have never

been there. You had me contemplating

the riddles of birds: *What looks open*

and invites you in but is something you can

never enter? You even had me laughing

at the jokes birds make, like the one

about the Northern Flicker that believes

the cup tattooed on his chest is half

full, when it's really half empty. You had me

at Andrei Rublev's grave, which no one

can find, although the bells keep

ringing anyway. Sitting next to you

on the bed before you left, you had me

sitting before the road and you had me inside

you leaving Venice, chanting with the novices

in the monastery of Grande Chartreuse: *Tu m'as*

séduit, o Seigneur, et moi, je me suis laissé

séduire, O Lord you have seduced

me, and I let myself

be seduced.

État présent de mon esprit:

What do birds talk about

before the sun even

rises? They say *voici*

the letter C and agree

that the Colosseum,

the whole open

world, should be known

as the *Comeandseeum,*

that the world is scarred,

sacred, with not even a *scherzo*

to scare me. We used to think

time moved like sheep

nibbling their way

to some mountain's peak

with only the occasional saint

ascending in his or her

private *ascenseur.* But in

Der Rosenkavalier, the aging

Marschellin says, “Sometimes

I get up in the middle

of the night and stop

all the clocks,” their hands still

pointing forever the way

the lines on a family tree

become a pedigree — *a pé de*

grue — certain as the standing foot

of a crane, although we ourselves

are more like Augustine’s

music: something that can occur

only in time, a song held together by

time, entirely in the present, composed

of memory and anticipation.

Lord Byron's grandfather, exploring

for the British Navy, named the atolls

of Napuka and Tepoto the *Islands of*

Disappointment because he could get

close enough to see them

but never come ashore. My father,

when I was a child,

would swim underwater

like a frog, carrying me with him

on his back as if I were

the dorsal fin of some

fin de siècle.

Ma devise:

In the photo, my mother and aunt arrive home
from shopping to our staged scene: chairs
and tables toppled, doilies draped
on kitchen counters and lamp shades
like the melting watches in Dali's
The Persistence of Memory. "What
in the world?" they exclaim, stalled
at the open door in their belted
Bermuda shorts, tucked-in sleeveless
blouses, and matching hair like the tight
poodle pelt on my Tiny Tears doll,
their arms raised in the air as if we had
pointed our cap guns and yelled, "This is
a stick-up," as if they had stepped over
the threshold of heaven and found it far
more dirty and disheveled than they
had been led to believe. At dusk,
glowing red lights and posters
for aperitifs — *Amer Picon, Lillet,*
Dubonnet — at the entrance to the Paris Metro
guard the threshold that leads
to the underworld, although at the gate
of Dante's Hell, we're told to *Abandon*
all hope. My mother never heard of
Charon but always said when I
cautioned her about what she was
eating, "Something's got to carry me
away from this world." It could be
the saxophone of John Coltrane
or a *trombone,* the perfect French word

for paperclip, just as a hyphen
becomes a *trait d'union.* For Abbot Suger
in Saint-Denis, the Gothic cathedral — its gold
chalice budding rubies, emeralds, stones
of celestial blue, its windows staining
light — was a hyphen to heaven, some hymn,
hymen, haven. The iris of the eyes
in ancient statues, it's what the mantles
of the Madonnas were painted with, once
more valuable than gold. And if it was
good enough for Tutankhamen, it's good
enough for me. Still deep in the teeth
of the medieval manuscript illuminator
who always licked the tip of her
paint brush to a point, and powdered
into Cleopatra's eyeshadow: some magic
incantation in five syllables like *open*
sesame — or the way we said it as
kids, *open says-a-me* — that unlocks
a sealed cave, the *bon mots, mots*
justes: lapis lazuli, the true blue
that never fades.

Solstice

Towards the end
of her life, my mother kept
saying *I'm going to be here*
as long as I'm supposed
to be, as long as the days
of June and as long as
Proust said a sentence needs

to be because it contains a
complete thought, and no matter
how complex it may be, the thought
should remain intact because the shape
of the sentence is the shape
of thought: think how
the hummingbird feeds as long

as it needs to, dipping
its tongue to make the nectar tremble,
although not nearly as long as I stayed
behind the Baptist church beneath
honeysuckle when I was ten, pulling
each flower's pistil back through
its throat to drip one sweet bead

onto my tongue before my parents
drove us up into the mountains
for the all-day meeting and supper
on the ground, which always
seemed to me more like all-day
supper with cakes and pies laid out, waiting
end-to-end on picnic tables, watermelons

soaking in their galvanized tubs
of ice while the grills kept burning
until even after evening
prayer, everyone still
had mustard on their
folded hands and
faces, the nights so dark

that all the fireflies were one
giant sparkler held up to tick away
the night in their hide-and-seek
here-I-am, over there, here, now
here, as if the shorter
the days become, the longer the sentence
needs to be.

The Swallows

out
wallow
the evening light
the
blue
borders the heart
needs
to leave. I waited
at a sign
said *B hold* — what
must have
been feeling

one's position
in the universe where
they met in secret
the "new bridge,"
which

puts
something hard

inside you the way
scientists knew they had discovered
blue whales
singing a song no one
heard.

Liaison

Michelangelo loved to touch and graze

the white shoulders of Carrara

and Pietrasanta, searching

for a block of marble that held

the body he would want

to release. But wouldn't it all

have been white and gray, perhaps

some blue, mostly blinding

in both summer and winter's

light? How many times

have you said that a vase

or some plate was blue, only

to hear your mother or lover say *no,*

it's green? What we all need

is a *nuancier,* what the French call

a color chart with its shades

of white or black or

blue, each with its own name — Alabaster,

Devon Cream, Delphinium, Deep

in Thought, Evening Dove, Amethyst

Shadow — as if a word were a leash

we could then unleash, or with which

we could even have a lease, not merely

a liaison. For that, you'd need to be

Michelangelo — or Proust, who

would know the favorite color

of the *me* in *Vermeer.* Ancient Romans

signed their name to a work

of art and then added the word

faciebat — third person singular imperfect

active indicative of the Latin verb *facere,*

to make. After his name

on the *Pietá* in St. Peter's,

Michelangelo carved

facieba, omitting the final letter *t*

and thus creating an imperfect form

of the imperfect, because he

believed, in keeping with Platonic

philosophy, that any work of art

never completely resembles

its heavenly counterpart, just as

my mother's perfumes — *White Shoulders,*

Joy — never completely

resembled her.

Devekut

One cleaves to God

through devout concentration

attuned to the divine veiled

presence immanent in all things. Even learning

must be interrupted in order to attain

this higher mystical state, so a Hasidic

master when studying a page of the Talmud

contemplates the white spaces

between black letters, just as

Piliated Woodpeckers prefer to knock

on trees where no one

is at home and leave holes

like the blanks in my father's unfinished

crossword puzzle. *46 Across: To be, below*

the Border shares an empty space

with *47 Down: Word attached to book,*

while all the squares of *48 Down: 'Theirs ______*

reason why,' Tennyson and *62 Across:*

With: Fr. are full. *Avec quoi?*

35 Across: Bei ___ Bist Du Schön

has to be *Mir.* We can follow

the tracks of the cloven-hooved deer

but still can't read what's quoted

between them, although I think

it would sound like the music I practiced

on the cardboard keyboard when I was

a child because we couldn't afford

a piano. Sometimes when playing a measure

of Beethoven, there is no note but

a chasm, which somehow still must be

played. Hiking the mountain trails

in Bavaria, everyone you encounter says

Grüss Gott, God greet you, and in the morning

each person who enters the breakfast room

says *Grüss Gott,* whether or not

there is anyone there.

Truly,

It was the best

worst times: every I

came back

along with

migrating birds that

crossed over

flying south tonight

at an attitude

of 1,700 feet

and a speed of 27 mph, while

waving

a dress onto an *almost.*

When

steps forward

before cutting a slit

up one leg from floor to thigh. Still,

so many questions: will I forever

or forever? And will forever be long enough

to light

the territory,

the way

to a heart.

For the Time Being,

my iPhone worked just fine, until it started
updating, installing new versions
of whichever version of iOS with which
it began — then soon began sending me
Memories: slideshows of photos accompanied

by music the phone itself had thought
appropriate to play along — as if my brain
were the trash dump of the ancient
Egyptian city of Oxyrhynchus, City of
the Sharp-Nosed Fish, where among the piles
of manuscripts, archeologists found

previously unknown lesbian erotica
by Sappho and fragments of the sayings
of Jesus, lying together. But how
can memory be so full of all the things
not in it — like the late December night

I stood in the driveway, hands shoved
in my jeans pockets, and laughed as you
drove down the street, car window open, yelling
I'm madly in love with you — not knowing I'd never
see you again. If only
memory would descend like snow
coming down on every side of Philip Johnson's
Glass House: he said that lying inside with
snow falling all around made it seem as if you were

rising on a "celestial elevator."

Ancient Romans clearly thought
that the dead were dead only
for the time being: 41 bent or twisted nails, unearthed
from a Roman tomb in a 2nd Century imperial
burial site, were meant to keep

the deceased in their place. And the statues
of emperors, still standing in Vaison la Romaine,
were built with heads that could easily
be replaced, although the statues
of lovers were never made
that way — as if memory, after all, might not be
a bug, but a feature.

Ce que je voudrais être: Fugue

Mother may I
moon glow, Mother may
I know who
bruised the moon, left
its scar on the back
of my arm like some
celestial heirloom. And who
crowned the White-crowned
Sparrow? Mother may I
take three giant steps
back, may I not
step on the crack that
breaks your back. May I
flee, take flight — *fugio,*
fugere — may I ride
autumn's sway and
drag, carry the dead
the way we carry
a tune. Mother may I push
the black button on top
of the Catbird's head. May I stay
in the Grand Hotel on
the Normandy coast and always
rent, like Proust, five expensive
rooms: one to live in
and four to contain
the silence. May I exit,
exist, Mother may I
leave the white space
between letters. In order to
grasp its prey, the tendons

of a hawk must contract
      its talons. In April, may
            the knuckles of peonies
know how
      to release.

She Said She Saw Vowels

underneath her birdfeeder
and that she wasn't sure
whether they were blind or just
had no eyes at all, but how
did they see where they were
going? Northern European
depictions of Christ being mocked
on his way to the cross show him
seated and blindfolded, but in
the small painting on wood panel
found hanging above the hotplate
of a ninety-four-year-old woman
selling off the contents of her home
in northern France, Christ stands
at the center beneath a gold leaf
sky, his eyes unmasked
in the Byzantine style. It sold at auction
for twenty-four million euros after tests
under infrared light revealed it was
painted by Cimabue in the thirteenth
century, the missing *volet gauche*
or left wing of a polyptych
altarpiece: tunnels made by worms in
its wood matched up with holes
in the other panels, indicating that they
were all once part of the same plank
of poplar. A 2016 study found
that voles are capable of empathy:
they comfort each other when
mistreated, spend more time grooming
an injured vole, and develop levels of

stress hormones similar to those
of voles that have been harmed.
Yet physicists tell us that dark matter
isn't matter, might not even
exist. It casts no shadow — like the *a*
in *after,* so there's no use
searching for its presence, only
its consequence, as with love when it's
over or the body deep in a grave,
which scientists now say continues
to move for over a year, but where
does it think it's going?

Pas Encore

The late summer

is never/after

being forced to

recant

and yet

the name of

your perfume

says *not yet,*　　the smallest

Paradise,　　the almost end

the only pink

I can find in this late fall.

Comment j'aimerais mourir:

in Old English *unweder,* "unweather,"
weather so extreme that it seems
to have come from another
climate or time, still holding
in my hand a lame, which bakers use
to carve their mark
on bread — not to be
confused with *l'âme,* the soul —
while blackbirds line up
to form an abacus on the wire
above me, listening
to the *Arpeggione Sonata,* which Schubert
composed for an almost
extinct instrument, like the moon
we keep singing to anyway — *Casta*
Diva, pure goddess, *shine*
on, shine on harvest moon
up in the sky (the most difficult
part of the opera, the soprano
replied, was not crying after
her own death) — and the moon, too,
a trace fossil, a sign left
by the impress of life rather than
life itself, as in the fitting
of a bespoke jacket: all dots
and dashes, Cézanne's
taches, what's left of Mont Sainte-
Victoire when he is done painting it.

Relais du Silence

When someone dies
in the Limousin region of France, they say
Il a laissé son écuelle, He has left his bowl, so a small
bowl is filled with Holy Water into which
an evergreen branch is dipped to bless
the body. After burial, they place the bowl
at the head of the tombstone: it can never
be used for anything else. My friend Jacqueline
says that some people insist
on a hierarchy of sorrows. If your
dog died after twenty years and my cat died
when I had lived with her for only three
months, who has the right to be
most sad? — which is like asking whose silence
is loudest: that of the blank sheet at the end
of *Finnegans Wake* or that of Joseph, who has not
one word recorded in the scriptures.
In Dawson City, the Klondike, cellulose nitrate
strips of silent film unspooled for years, waiting
for light, to tighten again around another reel.
Sometimes they would spontaneously
combust, burn down the theater
that held them, raging on even when
completely submerged in water. The French once
called their army *la grande muette, the great*
silent one, because they had to suffer
in silence, but in Dante's *Inferno,* the damned
suffer according to the principle of *contrapasso*
like the man in Missouri who killed
hundreds of deer and was sent to prison,
sentenced to watch, each week, the film
Bambi. Let us observe a moment of silence

and then book a room in the hotel
Relais du Silence, where we can engage
in Perpetual Adoration: human
trances, human nectars, ensuant
charm, a transhuman surname chant.
In the fresco at San Damiano, after the cross
speaks to St. Francis, St. Luke pours words
into the head of a smiling ox.

Scrittura Infinita

Leonardo did not like
to finish things, so his manuscripts remain
open, constantly postponing the idea
of an end, a conclusion, and when
his writings stopped in the middle
of a line or page, he added
a quivering line that looks

like a recording of small seismographic
tremors or the beating
of a heart. *Here,* I answered, when
they called my name
in kindergarten, the way
the Scarlet Tanager in the yew tree
says *here,* like Paris each time

I arrive. Leonardo thought that
to study the body is
to travel — *Mondo minore, Mondo*
maggiore — and compared his renderings
of human anatomy to Ptolemy's
maps of the cosmos. In one drawing,
the heart looks like a plant lifted

from its terracotta pot
in winter, roots clutching a frozen
plot of dirt, pruned stalks still
pointing up like St. John the Baptist
in Leonardo's painting. Tuscany
itself, birthplace of Leonardo, is the shape
of a badly drawn heart. *Here,* said my mother,

handing my father's glasses to
to the funeral director, asking
him to place them across
my father's eyes, as if in early summer,
late spring, the scribbled hills might
look back and say, *Ok, then, we're going on*
without you.

Slowly But Not Too Much

as if making your way through an alphabet

beginning with alpha, as if you stood in front
of the Arcimboldo paintings in Vienna and someone said

"*Spring* is in the Louvre, springtime is

in Paris." Sometimes we were word for word, sometimes

unspeakable like the painted stone angel

in Dijon, who has been grieving silently

over the Passion of Christ since the end

of the 14th/beginning of the 15th century, as if

someone had said to her, *adagio ma non tanto.* Think of

the joy of making it onto the train before
it departs — or the sudden blossom of what's possible

when you arrive a minute late and watch it
pull out of the station. Behind her,

the angel's wings remain unfurled

as if they might fly. She still

wears her favorite color: chipped-stone blue. My favorite

is *omega-may-I,* and yours: *Venetian-red-and-vanishing.*

When Your Lover Leaves You

Learn a language you've never heard

Plant ginkgo trees, which will drop
all of their leaves at once

Practice the duet St. Francis sang
with a nightingale

Replace mezuzah scripture at front door
with sentence from AI computer essay: *the present,*
like everything else, will soon come
to an end

Donate matching red leather women's World Champion
Ferrari Race-to-Win jackets

Touch the clothes left in the closet
the way the ocean plays tag
with the shore, and remember her design

for Lady Macbeth's dress: one thick red drip of
blood sewn in from waist to floor

Consider the difference between *remainder*
                    and *reminder*, forget

how she dropped all of her clothes
                    at once and left them
where they fell

Le pays où je désirerais vivre:

terra, *cara,* terroir: in the open
mouth of the wind, blue-black from all
the kites it has eaten, blown back
like the past, where the family lives
in Alexandre Dumas' *Le chevalier*
d'Harmental : 5 rue du Temps-Perdu.
In the about-to-bloom history
of wisteria, twisting while
the soft gray paws of pussy willow
boom suddenly above me, a thunderhead
nods like Mary at the Annunciation, recalling
how Abraham said the journey is within, from
inside us to inside us, *nous même à nous*
même. Where else could they be
headed in Tarkovsky's *Nostalghia* when
the chest of the Virgin Mary flies open
to release the beating doves?
Celtic *peregrini* wandered
in "thin places," sites in landscape
where the borders between
this place and some other, past
and present, feel most fragile, begin
to fray the way bison painted on walls
in the *Grotte de Niaux* move in
and out of rock as if it were
a membrane between worlds.
Out back,
the mourning dove bobbing
in the birdbath, one wing unfurled
and hoisted on its mast, doesn't even think
about sailing home. She's somewhere
between Pavlov and Pavlova.

Pas Encore

The late summer grasses say

not yet, which is never

the same as *nyet,* just as

Galileo, after being forced to

recant his claim that the Earth moves

around the sun, murmured

E pur si muove, and yet

it moves. Even the name of

your perfume, like the late summer

grasses, says *not yet,* but it's the smallest

island on the Seine that's named

Paradise, and at the almost end

of your breast is the only pink

I can find in this late fall.

Stars Roamed Above Us

trailing names we loved
to recite — even though their paths
looked brief as the crease in
the field made by deer passing
through or my reach across
you at night. So it's strange
to learn that *Earendel,* the oldest star
yet to be found
in the universe, has been trying
to reach us on Earth with its light
for thirteen billion years:
I thought stars
were asterisks, signs of something
missing or hidden like the row of
stars at login, standing in
for your password. What if the late
night sky is the color of eternity —
late teal — everyone adrift
and dressed in eclipse
plumage, chanting *While the moon is*
still stuck to the sky like a price tag, be my
rogue planet, my orphan star.

* * * * *

Every one of the ninety-four elements
found on Earth was created in
space: three during the first three minutes
of the birth of the universe, the rest
in cores of distant

stars. But if the calcium in our bones
and the iron in every cell of red blood
come from stars, when I desire
you, what do I desire? It's as you said:
when floating on your back
in the middle of the lake at night,
you can't tell the stars

* * * * *

from fireflies.

* * * * *

Even the strands of fungi
growing in the top four inches
of soil on Earth, linked end to end, would stretch
halfway across our galaxy.
Is that what they mean
by *desire lines?*
And are they the paths
we made, or only the ones
we wanted?

* * * * *

Strolling among paintings
in the Salon of 1767,
Diderot said, "I walk between
two eternities: the ruins of what was
and the ruins

* * * * *

of what will be."
They stopped mowing
the path through the tall meadow grass
where I first saw you. Eventually
the sheared sides moved back
together, not like the Red Sea after Moses
parted it — more like the part
in my hair that won't stay
where you put it.

The Woods Are Fond Always

It is the softest morning that ever I can

ever remember me. You

will tell me some time if I can believe its all.

If I ever. When the moon of mourning

is set and gone. Are

me not truly? It's

something fails us. First we

feel. Then we fall.

Shopping List for the Last Day on Earth in the Eternal City

Roman glass the color of eucalyptus

something hard, something voiced
between two vowels

a name for *Pas Encore Nommé* perfume

evening sky, even
Evensong

Bach's *St. Matthew Passion*
set on repeat

Givenchy L'Interdit

things not visible but about whose
position we are certain

Brodsky reading "Do Not Leave
the Room," set on repeat

the jokes birds make

things now useless that recall
a glorious past

wild geese flying through fog

the only pink I can find

a telephone connected
to nothing, nowhere

Clos de la Croix de Pierre Premier Cru

peonies from the *marché* in Paris

le pays où je désirerais vivre,
where you can find

what Pliny called something
of great rarity:

ptichye moloko, Russian bird's milk,
the milk that birds in Paradise

feed their young

the words *khochou tiebya,* want you
esche, more

Because

the nodding of the goldenrod, because
the season of squirrel with a nut in its mouth
because even the green rain of the river birch
eventually rusts, because in the Blue Ridge Mountains
there were places where paths and lanes crossed
and people gathered to dance by moonlight,
because swifts sleep high above the earth, one eye
closed and half the brain asleep as they fly
above the clouds, because Leonardo said
between shadows are other shadows
and Miles Davis sometimes turned his back
to the audience while playing in order to
better hear his horn, because Giambattista Vico
said *humanitas* "comes first and properly from
humando, burying," because everyone's hair grows
in a spiral even the crown of my mother's head
at 94 was a hurricane heading for some coast,
because Henry James saw sheep following
a shepherd down a twisting mountain path
"like the tail of a dingy comet," because birds
navigate by the stars, because for a good while
in the night two Barred Owls keep who-ing
each other but still don't know who's
going to cook dinner, because some things
are already ruins before they crumble, I leave
you, *ma biche,* with Chanel's *comète* necklace,
inspired by the Parisian sky, its trail of diamonds
slung around your neck.

Lost Again, *Monte Perdido, Mont Perdu,* Wherever

you're off to now, a single-strand pikake lei

swaying between breasts: *Aloha!* Just pretend

it's the transhumance, sheep threading their way

up your jagged crest in their grey woolly-rag

lollygag as if they were the basting stitch

of a god trying to figure out how to hold

everything together. The sheep, called *brebis*

on the French side of the border, pick their way

among stones littered along the peak where

someone must have emptied their pockets as if

it were a *vide-poche* tray, as if the sheep crept

in some trans-human trance across Germany

and Europe where the living step around to avoid

walking on the 40,000 permanent brass markers

embedded in the pavement: *stolpersteine,* stumbling

stones that announce where someone who was

murdered in the Holocaust once lived. When the sheep

look up, a bit of clipped grass remains

on each one's lip.

Remains

I can never remember whether
the saying goes "All roads lead
to Rome" or "All roads lead to
home," although if all roads do
lead to Rome, it makes sense that the road
to home would too, especially since
Romans built their roads on top of
older roads — the words *street* and *strada,* Latin
for roadway, come from
strata, layers — in the same way that
graves in the Old Jewish Cemetery
in Prague were stacked on top
of each other for centuries: as many as
twelve layers separated only
by a new heap
of soil. The Cinema Alberto Sordi
in Rome, suspended down into
the excavation site of medieval and
ancient ruins going back to the fourth
and fifth centuries — an extensive
network of shops, houses, streets — is wrapped
in windows: before the lights dim
and the show begins, moviegoers
can watch two thousand years
of history while Muscadet in the *Pays*
Nantais region of France ages
in subterranean glass-lined
tanks *sur lie* so that the wine
stays in contact with the dead
yeast cells for a fuller, richer
finish. Rising from ground that holds
a body, the headstone bears

its name as if it were staking some miner's
claim. The French have a word
for the descriptive text left in place
of art that has been
stolen: *fantôme,* left like her
tracks in new-fallen
snow or the lines of a poem heaped
one on top of another.

Before,

bees bumbled in hollyhock blossoms, minding
their own business, legs swaddled
in pollen. Some people believe
that chaffinches sing more sweetly after
being blinded, just as an empty room
sees all the things that once
were in it and the past keeps
the shape made
by lips saying *O*. Perhaps it's
heresay, although I say so

here: *Olyushka,* bespeak, be
chance, be siege, be
wilder, be loved,
bespoke, be
moan, as in
alpha, be fore
and aft, be cause and
effect as in *will you*
be come, be
hold, be *bop-a-lula, she's my*
baby: be a stanza
full of rooms, be
cause, caws,
the last thing uttered
by crows: a trampoline into the night.

Shopping List for Things Now Useless That Recall a Glorious Past

the small stones I will keep even though I no longer
remember where they came from

artillery balls and iron or stone bowls to grind
concave and convex lenses

a photo of the moon rising over the lagoon

something at a distance of nine miles appears as if it is
only one mile away

a song no one has heard

Galileo's shopping list for his trip to Venice:
pieces of mirror, lenses to make a more
powerful telescope

your words *let's not ever fight again*

the moons of Jupiter he discovered
with his new telescope

the *fur slippers and hat* that Galileo's son
has undoubtedly worn out by now

and the *ivory combs* which have lost their teeth

memory, the mast of a ship
diagonal in the sand

and Venice itself, of course — so many
bridges but which one to take

the domes of its churches still full
like breasts thrust into the morning sky

Eternity will be

that fondled them when they were Fire

will gleam and understand

To breathe my Blank without thee

Abbreviate me this

and this

gaze / for which / I cease to / live —

A fir / mament /for all

Afternoon and the West and

the gorgeous nothings

which compose the sunset keep

'No' is the wildest

word we consign

to Language

Notes

Sometime during 1889 or 1890, Marcel Proust responded to a questionnaire that was popular in France at the time. Proust titled his responses "Marcel Proust par lui-même" [Marcel Proust in his own words]. *Some of the topics he responded to are also the titles of the following poems:*

Le principal trait de mon caractère: My most striking trait
Le don de la nature que je voudrais avoir: The natural talent I'd like to have
État present de mon esprit: My spirit, right now
Ma devise: My motto
Ce que je voudrais être: What I'd like to be
Comment j'aimerais mourir: How I would like to die
Le pays où je désirerais vivre: The country where I want to live

"État present de mon esprit:" Comeandseeum: James Joyce's neologism for the Colosseum in Rome, in Stuart Gilbert, *Letters of James Joyce.*

"Ma devise:": Walter Benjamin, *The Arcades Project,* [C1a,2].

"Liaison": Paul Barolsky, *Michelangelo and the Finger of God.*

"Comment j'aimerais mourir:": With thanks to Martha Dana Rust.

"Relais du Silence": A French hotel chain promising quiet and tranquility.

"Slowly But Not Too Much": "*Spring* is in the Louvre ... " is from the film *Museum Hours.*

"When Your Lover Leaves You": The AI sentence is from the essay "The Future of Humanity," composed by OpenAI research institute's GPT-3 natural language processor.

"Shopping List for the Last Day on Earth in the Eternal City": Olga Maslova, *Last Day in the Eternal City* (oratorio).

"The Woods are Fond Always": A cento from Anna Livia's soliloquy in James Joyce's *Finnegans Wake*.

"Shopping List for Things Now Useless That Recall a Glorious Past": Sei Shōnagon, *The Pillow Book*, 11th Century AD; Galileo Galilei's shopping list, August 1609; Galileo, letter to the Doge of the Republic of Venice, August 24, 1609.

"Eternity will be": A cento composed from Emily Dickinson's letters, poems, and poems written on envelopes.

Acknowledgements

Copper Nickel: "Inside Hagia Sophia," *"Le don de la nature que je voudrais avoir:"*

FIELD: "Remains"

The Gettysburg Review: "Shopping List for Things Now Useless That Recall a Glorious Past"

Great River Review: "Solstice," *"Le pays où je désirerais vivre:" "Comment j'aimerais mourir:"*

Harvard Review: "The Swallows Come Out," "Stars Roamed Above Us"

Interim: "Relais du Silence," "Lost Again, *Monte Perdido, Mont Perdu,* Wherever," *"Pas Encore"*

The Manhattan Review: "Dark Matter," "Spring"

The Massachusetts Review: "Liaison"

New American Writing: "Yours truly," "Privilege for the vocabulary"

Peripheries: "You Had Me at *Premier Cru*"

Plume: "She Said She Saw Vowels," "Slowly But Not Too Much," "When Your Lover Leaves You"

Plume Featured Selection, "Marcel Proust's Questionnaire: A Sequence": *"Le principal trait de mon caractère:" "Le don de la nature que je voudrais avoir:"* (reprint) *"État présent de mon esprit:" "Ma devise:" "Ce que je voudrais être:* Fugue" *"Comment j'aimerais mourir:"* (reprint) *"Le pays où je désirerais vivre"* (reprint)

Plume Poetry Anthology 7: Featured poet: *"Devekut"*

Revel: "The Present," "Because" (reprint), "You Had Me at *Premier Cru*" (reprint), "Solstice" (reprint)

Seneca Review: "I Can't See the Hour"

Unbound Edition Press (anthology), *The Experiment Will Not Be Bound:* "Because"

Frontispiece photo: *Aphrodite of Menophantos,* Museo Nazionale Romano Palazzo Massimo alle Terme. Photo by Slava Shvets.

My thanks to Martha Collins, Janice N. Harrington, Mark Irwin, Christopher Kempf, J. Allyn Rosser, and Corey Van Landingham, and enduring gratitude to David Walker and David Young.

I'm grateful to the James Merrill House committee and community for the James Merrill House Writer-in-Residence fellowship — and to Willard Spiegelman for his support of my work from the beginning.

To Patrick Davis and Peter Campion: your vision and kindness are truly unbound.

About the Author

Angie Estes is the author of seven books of poems. *Enchantée,* won the 2015 Kingsley Tufts Poetry Prize and the Audre Lorde Prize for Lesbian Poetry, and *Tryst* was selected as one of two finalists for the 2010 Pulitzer Prize. Her second book, *Voice-Over,* won the 2001 *FIELD* Poetry Prize and was also awarded the 2001 Alice Fay di Castagnola Prize from the Poetry Society of America. Her first book, *The Uses of Passion* (GibbsSmith, 1995), was the winner of the Peregrine Smith Poetry Prize. A collection of essays devoted to Estes' work appears in the University of Michigan Press "Under Discussion" series: *The Allure of Grammar: The Glamour of Angie Estes's Poetry* (2019).

The recipient of many awards, including a Guggenheim Fellowship, a Pushcart Prize and the Cecil Hemley Memorial Award from the Poetry Society of America, she has also received fellowships, grants, and residencies from the National Endowment for the Humanities, the National Endowment for the Arts, the Woodrow Wilson Foundation, the American Academy in Rome, the Lannan Foundation, the California Arts Council, the Illinois Arts Council, and the Ohio Arts Council. In 2023, she was a Writer-in-Residence Fellow at the James Merrill House.

About the Type and Paper

Designed by Malou Verlomme of the Monotype Studio, Macklin is an elegant, high-contrast typeface. It has been designed purposely for more emotional appeal.

The concept for Macklin began with research on historical material from Britain and Europe dating to the beginning of the 19th century, specifically the work of Vincent Figgins. Verlomme pays respect to Figgins's work with Macklin, but pushes the family to a more contemporary place.

This book is printed on natural Rolland Enviro Book stock. The paper is 100 percent post-consumer sustainable fiber content and is FSC-certified.

Last Day on Earth in the Eternal City was designed by Eleanor Safe and Joseph Floresca.

Unbound Edition Press champions honest, original voices. Committed to the power of writers who explore and illuminate the contemporary human condition, we publish collections of poetry, short fiction, and essays. Our publisher and editorial team aim to identify, develop, and defend authors who create thoughtfully challenging work which may not find a home with mainstream publishers. We are guided by a mission to respect and elevate emerging, under-appreciated, and marginalized authors, with a strong commitment to advancing LGBTQ+ and BIPOC voices. We are honored to make meaningful contributions to the literary arts by publishing their work.

unboundedition.com